ENERGY
ALL AROUND

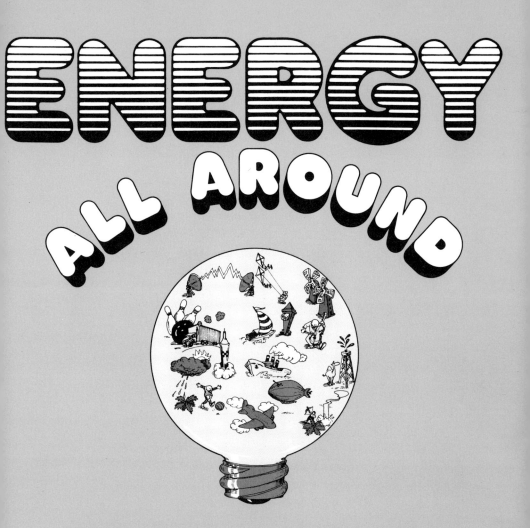

by Tillie S. Pine and Joseph Levine

ILLUSTRATED BY JOEL SCHICK

MCGRAW-HILL BOOK COMPANY

NEW YORK   ST. LOUIS   SAN FRANCISCO   DÜSSELDORF
JOHANNESBURG   KUALA LUMPUR   LONDON   MEXICO
MONTREAL   NEW DELHI   PANAMA   RIO DE JANEIRO
SINGAPORE   SYDNEY   TOKYO   TORONTO

also by Tillie S. Pine and Joseph Levine

THE AFRICANS KNEW
THE CHINESE KNEW
THE EGYPTIANS KNEW
THE ESKIMOS KNEW
THE INDIANS KNEW
THE PILGRIMS KNEW
THE INCAS KNEW
THE MAYA KNEW
THE POLYNESIANS KNEW
AIR ALL AROUND
ELECTRICITY AND HOW WE USE IT
FRICTION ALL AROUND
GRAVITY ALL AROUND
HEAT ALL AROUND
SIMPLE MACHINES AND HOW WE USE THEM
ROCKS AND HOW WE USE THEM
WATER ALL AROUND
WEATHER ALL AROUND
MEASUREMENTS AND HOW WE USE THEM

234567RABP789876

Library of Congress Cataloging in Publication Data

Pine, Tillie S
  Energy all around.

  SUMMARY: Describes the sources and uses of
various kinds of energy and the need for energy
conservation.
    1. Power resources—Juvenile literature.
  2. Power (Mechanics)—Juvenile literature.
  [1. Power resources.   2. Force and energy]
  I. Levine, Joseph, 1910-   joint author.
  II. Schick, Joel.   III. Title.
  TJ163.2.P56   333.7   75-15069
  ISBN 0-07-050087-8

TO
VICTOR AND STEPHANIE

WHOSE ABUNDANCE OF CREATIVE ENERGY
IS SURELY AMAZING

WHAT IS ENERGY?

What makes it possible for—
  cars and trucks to move,
  trains to run,
  ships to sail,
  jet planes to take off,
  water wheels to turn,
  bells to ring,
  and—
  for you to run, jump, work and play?

This book will tell you—
  what energy is,
  how energy changes,
  where the fuel for energy comes from,
  and—
  how energy makes it possible
  for us to do the things we do.

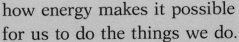

WHERE DOES ENERGY COME FROM?

Throw a ball into the air!

What makes the ball go up?
Your moving arm does.

Kick a football!

What makes the football fly off?
Your moving leg does.

Drop a pebble into a tub of water!

What makes the water ripple?
The moving pebble does.

Shoot an arrow at a target!

What makes the arrow shoot out?
The moving string of the bow does.

Do you see that moving things have
the *ability* to make other things move?

We call this ability—*ENERGY!*

So —
your moving arm, your moving leg, the moving pebble,
the moving string — all have energy in them.

And —
when these things move, we say they have
moving energy.

Things in motion can make other things move.

So —
your moving arm moves the ball,
your moving leg moves the football,
the moving pebble moves the water,
the moving string moves the arrow.

In the same way,
falling rain can make leaves move,
falling rocks can push other rocks downhill,
strong winds can blow hats off,
moving water can turn water wheels,
and—when you hit a marble with your "shooter,"
that marble, too, moves.

Now you know that—
when one thing moves, it can make a second
thing move. When this happens, we say that the
moving energy of the first thing is *transferred*
to the second thing.

And now—
the second thing has moving energy of its own.

Do you think that this second moving thing
can make a third thing move, too? Try it.

Where is moving energy transferred
in each picture?

Do this.

Push a pencil across the top of a table.
Your moving hand makes the pencil move.

Now—
push hard against the wall of your room.
Keep pushing!
Do you move the wall? Of course not!

When you push the pencil, the pencil moves
and energy is transferred from you to the pencil.

When this happens, we say that you are doing *work*.

Are you doing work when you push against the wall?
No, you are not
because—
you do *not* make the wall move.
Work is done *only* when something is moved—when
it is pushed, pulled or lifted.

Is work done when —
   a sailboat glides across a lake,
   a wave knocks you down,
   mother knits a sweater,
   baby shakes a rattle,
   a car pulls a trailer,
   a horse pulls a carriage,
   you pick up a pin from the floor?

Work is done only when something is moved.
Energy makes things move.
Energy can be transferred to make other things move.

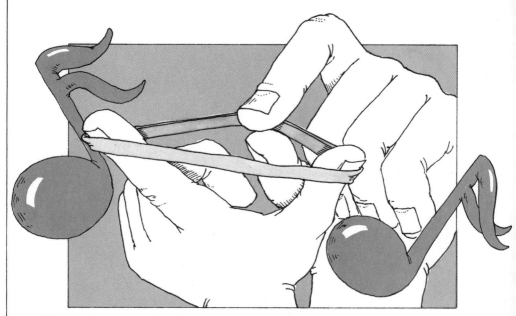

HOW DOES ENERGY CHANGE?

Stretch a rubberband between your thumbs and pluck it.

Do you see the rubberband vibrate quickly?
Do you hear the sound it makes?
How do these things happen?

When you pluck the rubberband, energy is transferred from you to the rubberband.
The rubberband vibrates quickly—so quickly that it makes sound waves that travel through the air.

So—the moving energy of the rubberband
makes the air around it vibrate
and—you hear this vibrating air as sound.

Now do this:

Rest the side of your head on a table.
Stretch out your arm and tap the table with your
fingers. Do you hear the sound? The tapping
makes the table top vibrate quickly—
so quickly that you hear the vibrations
through the table top as sound even though
you do *not* see the vibrations.

Place your fingers on the front of your throat.
You do *not* feel any vibrations.

Now—sing a song! Talk! Do you feel the
vibrations in your throat? You certainly do!

When you sing or speak, air moves in your throat
and makes your vocal cords vibrate quickly—
so quickly that they make the vibrations
you hear as sound.

What is vibrating quickly in each picture to make the sound?

How is moving energy changed to sound in each of these pictures?

Rub your hands together quickly and hard.

Do you hear the sound of rubbing?

The moving energy of your hands rubbing against each other makes the air vibrate. You hear these vibrations as sound.

But—do your rubbing hands also feel warm?
Yes, they do. Why?

All things are made up of tiny, tiny bits called *molecules*. These molecules keep moving around. When you rub your hands together, the rubbing makes the molecules move faster and—the faster the molecules move, the warmer your hands feel. So—the moving energy of your rubbing hands changes into *heat* energy.

Whenever things rub together, moving energy changes to heat energy.

Who knows this?

Mechancis do. They know that the moving parts in engines can get very hot. So—the mechanics oil these parts to make the rubbing smoother and to keep the engines from overheating.

Space scientists do. They know that when their space ships re-enter the air from outer space at terrific speeds, the space ships *could* burn up from rubbing against the air. So—they put shields of special materials on the crafts to prevent the ships from burning up.

Baseball players do. They wear pads on their thighs. These pads prevent skin burns when the players slide into base.

Now—turn the wheel of a toy sparkler.
The moving energy of your fingers makes the wheel
move. The moving energy of the turning wheel makes
the sound you hear.

The turning wheel does something else. It rubs
against the flint in the sparkler. This metal rubbing
against the flint makes the sparks of light you see.
How does this happen?

When the moving wheel rubs against the flint,
tiny bits of flint rub off and fly out. These
rubbed-off pieces are hot—so hot that they glow
and send off light waves. You see the sparks.

In this way, moving energy changes into *heat* energy
and then into *light* energy.

Did you ever see a train start to move?
Sometimes the turning wheels turn a bit too fast
on the rails and—sparks fly!

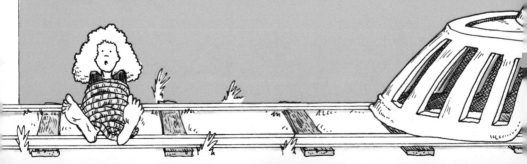

Do you know why?

Sometimes the engineer tries to stop a fast-moving train very quickly by jamming on the brakes and— sparks fly!

Do you know why?

So you see—
moving energy can change into sound, heat and light energy.

In each picture, moving energy changes into
another kind of energy. What kind of energy is that?

Would you be surprised to learn that there is a kind of energy in your rubber ball even when you are holding it in your hand? We say that the ball has the *ability* to make something move when you want to use that ability. We might say that it has *hidden* energy.

How can you make this hidden energy of the ball become moving energy to make something else move?

Throw your ball at an empty tin can.
    What happens when your moving ball hits the can?
    The can moves!

So you see—
when you throw the ball, you make hidden energy become moving energy and—this moving energy moves the can.

Who knows that there is hidden energy in things?

People who sail sailboats do. They know that their sailboats will move across the water *only* when the wind blows.

People who own windmills do. They know that
their windmills will turn and help them grind
their grain *only* when the wind blows.

Divers do. They know that they will be pushed
up into the air when they dive, *only* when they make
the springboard move down to push them up.

You do. You know that your friend on the other end
of the seesaw will go up *only* when you go down.

So you see—there is hidden energy in many things.

Can you think of other things that have hidden
energy in them that can become moving energy?

ENERGY ALL AROUND

If there were no energy, nothing
could move and no work could be done.

But—there *is* energy!

Where does almost all of this energy come from?

It comes from the sun!

The sun shines on the Earth and everything on it—
the waters, the air, the lands, the plants, the animals—
all take in or absorb energy from the sun.

What happens when water absorbs energy
from the sun?

To help you understand, do this:

Place two saucers of water in the sunlight.
Cover one saucer. Do not cover the other. After
two days, look at each saucer. What do you find?

You find that the water in the uncovered
saucer has almost disappeared. The water in the
covered saucer is still there.

Where did the water in the uncovered saucer
go? It went into the air.
The sun's energy helped to *evaporate* the water.

In the same way, the sun's energy helps to
evaporate water from the oceans, lakes and rivers.
The evaporated water becomes moisture in the air
and rises. This helps make clouds, rain and snow.

Rain and melting snow help make the flowing
streams and rivers and—
we use the power of these flowing streams and
rivers to turn water wheels that do work for us.

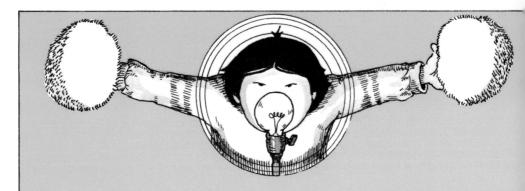

What happens when air absorbs energy from the sun?

Do this:

Sprinkle some powder on two powder puffs.
Hit the puffs together. What do you see?
The powder falls to the floor.

Hold your hand near a lighted bulb.
You feel the heat because the heated bulb warms
the air around it. Now—hit the puffs together gently
above the lighted bulb. What do you see this time?
Some of the powder rises. This happens
because the warmed air around the hot bulbs rises
and carries some of the powder with it.

So—
the energy of the rising air is transferred
to the powder and makes it rise too.

In the same way—
the sun's energy warms up the air around
the Earth. The warm air rises. The energy
of this moving air helps make more air move around.

This moving air is the *wind*. We use
the push of winds to turn windmills. We also
use the wind to push sailboats and to fly our kites.

What happens when plants absorb energy from the sun?

Get two small potted plants. Put one in the sunlight and the other in a dark closet. After several days, look at each plant. You will see that the plant in the sunlight looks fresh and the other plant looks wilted. Why did this happen?
The sunlight helped the first plant to stay fresh and healthy. Without sunlight, the leaves of the second plant wilted.

In the same way, the sun shines on the plants and trees of the Earth and helps keep them healthy. The leaves make starch and sugar—the *food* energy that plants and trees need to grow.

In this way, plants and trees have the sun's energy stored in them.

Do *you* use this stored energy?

Yes, you do—because the food you eat comes from plants and animals that have the sun's energy stored in them.

So—
when you eat vegetables and cereals, milk and fruit, meat and fish, your body changes the stored energy into body energy.

And—when you
   walk and run,
   read and write,
   blow a horn,
   hit a ball,
you are using your body energy to help you do these things and everything else that you do every day.

How do we use the stored energy of trees?

If you live in a house with a fireplace,
put some paper and logs in the fireplace.

Light the paper under the logs.
The logs catch fire. Why?

The logs are cut-up tree trunks. You know that
there is stored energy in the wood logs.
When the logs get hot enough, they start to burn.
The stored energy in the logs changes into
heat energy and you have a wood fire in your fireplace.

How else do we use the stored energy of trees?

For millions of years, trees and plants
have fallen in forests. These fallen trees and plants
were pressed farther and farther down into the earth.
Slowly, slowly the buried trees and plants changed
into black rocks.

What happened to the stored energy of the trees
and plants? It remained stored in the black rocks.

One day, men dug into the earth and discovered
this buried energy.

They found coal!

And—
when we burn coal, the stored energy of the coal
changes to heat energy.

Who uses the heat energy of burning coal?

Superintendents of some buildings do. They
burn coal in furnaces to make steam for heating
the buildings.

Manufacturers of steel do. They burn coal
in their gigantic ovens to get enough heat to make
iron and steel.

Some railroad engineers do. They burn coal in the
locomotive engines to make steam to drive the trains.

So you see—
when we burn wood and coal, we are really using
the stored energy of trees and plants for fuel.

There is another kind of stored energy we use for fuel.
It, too, comes from deep, deep down in the Earth.

For millions and millions of years, when plants
and animals died, they, too, were pressed down
deep into the earth. Slowly, slowly they changed
their form and became a dark, heavy liquid.

What happened to the stored energy of these plants
and animals? It remained stored in this liquid.
Then, one day, men dug into the earth and
discovered this buried energy. The found *crude oil*!

We call this oil *petroleum*.

Scientists have found out how to get many
different kinds of fuel oils, such as gasoline and
kerosene, from petroleum and—when we burn these fuel
oils, the stored energy of the oils changes to heat energy.

Wherever petroleum is found, we often find
another kind of buried energy—*natural gas*.
We pipe out this gas and use it, too, as a fuel
for burning.

These pictures show some of the fuels made from petroleum and how they are used.

There is another kind of energy we use
only when we want to use it.

Turn the switch of your lamp.
The light goes on.

Toast a slice of bread.
The hot bread pops up.

Turn on your radio.
You hear the music.

Turn on your TV set.
You hear and see the program.

Switch on your air conditioner.
You feel the cool air blowing.

What makes all these things happen?
Electrical energy does!

When you turn on the switches, electricity
flows through wires and—
    lights shine,
    toasters get hot,
    radios and TV's play,
    motors run.

Where does electricity come from?

Most of our electricity is made by burning fuel oil
in large burners to boil water to make steam. We also
burn coal to do this.

We are even trying to use the burnable material found
in collected garbage as fuel to help make steam.

The hot steam rushes through pipes to turn huge
wheels called turbines. The moving energy of the
spinning turbines turns other huge machines called
generators and—the moving energy of the generators
makes *electrical energy.*

We make some electricity by building huge concrete dams across rivers to form large lakes. We put big pipes into the dams and build turbines in the power houses of these dams.

The moving energy of the water rushing through the pipes turns the turbines and the spinning turbines turn the generators to make electricity.

Electrical energy flows through wires into your home. When you want to use this energy, you turn the switch "on." When you do not want to use this energy, you turn the switch "off."

Who are some of the people who use
electrical energy?

Carpenters—when they use power tools to
help them cut and smooth wood.

Factory workers—when they use electrical machines
of all kinds to help them do their work.

Automobile makers—when they use machines to
make parts and to assemble cars.

People in cities and towns—when they light
up the streets, highways and airports.

Advertising people—when they want their signs
to shine at night.

Father—when he uses an electric shaver.

Mother—when she uses her electric sewing machine.

How can we use the energy of the sun's rays
as a fuel?

On a sunny day, when there is no wind, put
a few scraps of tissue paper into a dish and place
the dish outside in the sunshine. Hold a magnifying glass
about twelve inches away from the dish, so that the
sun shines through the glass and onto the paper.

Move the magnifying glass slowly back and
forth until the sun's rays make a very small spot
of light on the tissue paper. What happens? The
paper begins to burn. (Make sure that the paper
burns itself out completely.)

In this way, you used the sun's rays directly
as a fuel to get enough heat to make a small fire.
You used *solar energy* as a fuel!

Some people in many parts of the world are
beginning to collect solar energy in large glass or
metal panels, and to use it as fuel to heat houses.

Some people are also using solar energy to make electrical
power to run machines.

Can you believe that scientists are now using
solar panels in space ships to collect the sun's energy?
This energy is used to keep charging the batteries that
make the electricity needed to run the space ships.

Scientists are also using another kind of
energy to make electricity—*atomic energy!*

They have learned how to use the heat energy
of atomic fuels such as *uranium* and *plutonium*.

They put these materials into special huge machines
called reactors, and use the tremendous heat given
off by these fuels to boil water to make steam.

They use the energy of steam to make electricity
and to run different kinds of engines.

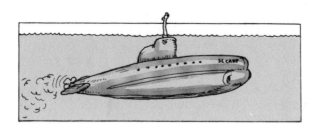

The propellers of this submarine are turned by engines using atomic energy.

The propellers of this ship are turned by an engine using atomic energy.

This generator is run by atomic energy to make electricity.

Scientists are now working on ways to make small atomic energy engines and to use the power of these engines to run airplanes, trains, machines in factories and even automobiles and trucks.

People all over the world are now talking
about an "Energy Crisis."
What do they mean by this?

They *really* mean that we are using up the Earth's wood,
coal, petroleum and natural gas too quickly and
that we may even run out of these fuels some day.
What can we do about this?
Everybody has to learn how to keep from
wasting these fuels.

You know that our scientists have found out
how to use different kinds of energy for the power
to do our work.

But—the scientists know that we need
still more energy to get more power.

So—
they are searching for new ways of using
the energy of the wind, of the heat in the Earth,
of the sun and of the atom.

Perhaps when you grow up, you will want to
help them in this search.